Tasters and Partakers

Dag Heward-Mills

Parchment House

Unless otherwise stated, all Scripture quotations are taken from the King James Version of the Bible.

TASTERS AND PARTAKERS

Copyright © 2022 Dag Heward-Mills

First published 2022 by Parchment House

Find out more about Dag Heward-Mills at:

Healing Jesus Campaign
Email: evangelist@daghewardmills.org
Website: www.daghewardmills.org
Facebook: Dag Heward-Mills
Twitter: @EvangelistDag

ISBN : 978-1-64330-601-8

All rights reserved under international copyright law. Written permission must be secured from the publisher to use or reproduce any part of this book.

Contents

1. What It Means to be a Taster 1
2. What It Means to Become a Partaker 10

CHAPTER 1

What It Means to be a Taster

O TASTE AND SEE THAT THE LORD IS GOOD;
How blessed is the man who takes refuge in Him!

Psalm 34:8 (NASB)

There is a big difference between tasting something and actually partaking in something. God wants you to partake of the great things that He has made available to you in the ministry.

To taste something is to nibble at it or to try it on your tongue. This little book is about serving God beyond the level of a taster.

Having a taste of something does not mean that you actually partake of it. There are some fast-food restaurants that give you a sample of what they are selling on a toothpick. They want you to have a small bite and eat a small amount so that you experience a sensation of what the real thing would be like.

God is great! It is not enough to just be aware of His existence and to think about Him. The ministry of the Lord Jesus Christ is the greatest job a human being can ever be involved with. It is not enough to taste the ministry or to be familiar with little aspects of it. There are many higher realms and deeper depths to everything in the ministry.

> **But Jonathan heard not when his father charged the people with the oath: wherefore he put forth the end of the rod that was in his hand, and dipped it in an honeycomb, and put his hand to his mouth; and his eyes were enlightened. Then answered one of the people, and said, Thy father straitly charged the people with an oath, saying, Cursed be the man that eateth any food this day. And the people were faint. Then said Jonathan, My father hath troubled the land: see, I pray you, how mine eyes have been enlightened, because I tasted a little of this honey.**
>
> **1 Samuel 14:27-29**

In the story above, King Saul cursed anyone who would eat that day. Jonathan, the son of King Saul got into trouble because he tasted a little bit of honey.

Then Saul said to Jonathan, Tell me what thou hast done. And Jonathan told him, and said, I did but taste a little honey with the end of the rod that was in mine hand, and, lo, I must die. And Saul answered, God do so and more also: for thou shalt surely die, Jonathan. And the people said unto Saul, SHALL JONATHAN DIE, who hath wrought this great salvation in Israel? GOD FORBID: as the LORD liveth, there shall not one hair of his head fall to the ground; for he hath wrought with God this day. SO THE PEOPLE RESCUED JONATHAN, THAT HE DIED NOT.

1 Samuel 14:43-45

Somehow Jonathan escaped execution because he only tasted the honey. The people rescued him from the curse because he had just tasted the honey and not partaken of it. Being a taster is different from being a partaker. The experiences of a taster are different from those of a partaker.

When you are a taster, you are more of an observer and a sympathiser than a partaker of the real thing. You may even have a level of understanding and be able to give advice and comments. But it does not mean that you are a partaker. In many organisations, there are people who are members of a board that gives non-binding comments and non-binding advice to the real executive management. At the end of the day, it is the executive management who are partaking of the actual running of the organisation.

A passenger on a ship is a taster of what goes on, on a ship. A captain of a ship is a real partaker of a sailor's job. Sitting on the outside and passing remarks about the running of a large ship is different from being the captain of the ship. Making comments about how things are being done is different from being involved in navigating and steering a ship. Managing a thousand employees on board a ship is different from making comments about how to run a ship. There is a big difference between a partaker and a taster. Are you a taster or a partaker?

It is time to become a real partaker of ministry.

Are you a Taster of the Ministry?

> **And the house of Israel called the name thereof Manna: and it was like coriander seed, white; and the TASTE OF IT WAS LIKE WAFERS MADE WITH HONEY.**
>
> **Exodus 16:31**

1. **A taster is a person who has had a little experience of ministry.**

   If you are a lay person, you have had a very small and limited experience of ministry.

2. **A taster is a person who has seen a little bit of ministry.**
   Ministering in your own country will give you only a small taste of ministry. When you travel to other countries you will discover other dimensions of ministry that you did not know before.

3. **A taster is a person who has sampled the ministry.**

   It is a privilege to be a pastor of a church. Being a pastor of a small church makes you a taster of pastoral work. When your church has not grown beyond a hundred members, you are simply a taster of the pastoral ministry. It will taste like the wafers of honey and you will have a sense of what ministry is like. I can tell you it is more thrilling to be a pastor of a large congregation than a pastor of a small congregation.

   One day, I transferred a pastor of a small congregation to a much larger church. He was thrilled as he had the opportunity to preach to many more people. What a difference it was for him to see people responding in large numbers to his powerful teachings. I have been a pastor of many little groups. For many years, I have had the privilege of talking to twenty people, forty people, sixty people and eighty people. I was so excited when our church crossed the seventy mark. Most churches do not grow beyond seventy people. I remember standing in the Olympic Stadium in Seoul, Korea, preaching to a hundred thousand people. What a privilege it was to enjoy and partake of a higher level of ministry.

4. **A taster is a person who has had a brief encounter with ministry.**

If you have been in full time ministry for just two or three years, you have had a brief encounter with real ministry. You need to stay in the ministry for ten years, fifteen years, twenty years and more. It is nice that you have started out and have spent two years of your life working in the ministry. But that is just a brief encounter. Many things happen as time goes by.

In a brief encounter, you will not be offended. As the years go by, you will definitely be offended. Jesus predicted that offences would surely come. This means that it is a matter of time until you are hurt by something. Jesus actually said that offences were necessary. Why are offences necessary? Because they mature you and they baptize you into the realities that exist in this world.

Woe unto the world because of offences! for it must needs be that offences come; but woe to that man by whom the offence cometh!

Matthew 18:7

When you become a partaker of the ministry, you will partake of the hurt and the offences that characterise real ministry. If you are able to survive your hurts and offences then you can become a true partaker.

5. **A taster of ministry is a Christian who is slightly acquainted with ministry.**

Being an acquaintance is different from being a friend. An acquaintance is someone you know but who is not a close friend. When you are a taster of ministry, you are in it but you are not close. When you are close, there are always more things that you know, see and feel. When you are close you join the decision-making process. When you are a taster, you hear about the decisions and receive announcements. When you are deeply involved, you see the tension and feel the stress that goes on behind the scenes.

6. **A taster is a person who has some awareness, some knowledge and some experience of ministry.**

Indeed, a taster is often deceived because he has some knowledge and some experience. But there is much more.

When I started playing golf, my caddy remarked that my golf would never improve if I played once a week. I was shocked when he said that.

I thought to myself, "He cannot be right." But he insisted that anyone who played once a week was just a taster. Indeed, I was just a taster of the golf game. Later on, I found out that there were people who played golf every single day of their lives. I also found out that there were people who practiced their golf swing every day by hitting hundreds of shots with the same club from the same position. And I found out that there were people who practiced by putting one thousand balls a day. Then I met someone who told me that he played eighteen holes in the morning and eighteen holes in the evening every day. More and more I realised that I was a taster of golf and not a partaker.

Tasters are filled with ignorance and pride. I was a taster and I had no idea about how far I was from actually partaking in this amazing game of golf. I was simply a taster because I was playing golf once a week.

In the same way, many lay pastors are deceived and proud because they have some knowledge and some limited experience in ministry. They have no idea of the extent of the work that goes on behind the scenes. In my ministry, there is endless work from morning till evening. All kinds of activities and all varieties of work go on every day to the point where people have to be compelled to take a day off.

It is important to understand when you are simply a taster of ministry and not actually a partaker. Understanding that you are simply a taster will cause you to have the humility to seek to know more. I once spoke to a lay pastor who worked for the government. I asked him if he would be interested in working in the ministry. He answered, "If there is something to do then I will be ready to work for the Lord." This was an unfortunate answer because it showed his ignorance about real ministry. He was a taster of the ministry who was being invited to be a partaker.

Today, there are many tasters out there who must face the fact that there is something higher, greater and deeper to partake of.

7. A taster is a person who has enjoyed the ministry to a point.

As the apple tree among the trees of the wood, so is my beloved among the sons. I sat down under his shadow with great delight, AND HIS FRUIT WAS SWEET TO MY TASTE.

Song of Songs 2:3

Bearing fruits in God, no matter how small, is sweet to the taste. His fruit will always be sweet to the taste. O taste and see that the Lord is good! But there is even more sweetness and joy when you are a partaker of the ministry.

There is great joy in serving God. Indeed, the joy that comes as you serve the Lord is something that is not easily explained. Many people who work as volunteers have the joy of the Lord as they serve Him. But there is a deeper joy in going all out and becoming an actual partaker of ministry.

O, what joy I have experienced serving the Lord in full-time ministry for many years! In all the years that I have worked in the ministry, I have never felt like going home early and getting away from the work. I have never wanted to know when vacation was beginning.

When I worked in the secular world, I was always counting the number of leave days I was entitled to. I was an expert at connecting my leave days with other public holidays and weekends, in order to create an extended holiday for myself. I hated secular work and enjoyed being a lay pastor. But when I came to work for the Lord in full-time ministry, I had much more joy and peace. The enjoyment that is found in serving the Lord all the time can never be compared with working for the Lord on Tuesday evenings and Sunday mornings.

8. Being a taster makes you proud about what you think you know.

A taster can express an opinion about the ministry because a taster does have some insight into the ministry. A taster must not think he knows everything because he actually knows very little.

I remember when a young man met one of my pastors and asked him what exactly he did in the office. He could not understand what he did from morning till evening every day. I understood why he was puzzled. I also do not understand what people do in banks from morning till evening. If they just give out loans, what else is there to do that keeps so many hidden people working on so many floors, in these glassy skyscraper banks?

It is the same kind of question that people ask about housewives. "What exactly does a housewife do all day?" It is because you have little insight to what it takes to look after a home that you think a housewife has nothing much to do. Perhaps you are just a taster of housework but not a partaker. You may not know what is involved in cooking and cleaning.

A taster is someone who is sympathetic to the work but has done very little himself. A taster is ignorant of the extent of work that takes place to make things work.

I once stumbled into a kitchen where I saw raw meat with blood all over it. I was horrified. "What is happening here?" I asked myself. I simply did not realise that the nice food I was eating came out of this "slaughterhouse" environment. It is important for us to go deeper and become partakers. Otherwise, we will make comments that reveal our emptiness.

CHAPTER 2

What it Means to Become a Partaker

For we have become PARTAKERS of Christ if we keep the beginning of our commitment firm until the end,

Hebrews 3:14 (NASB)

To become a partaker is to become many things. In this chapter, you will discover many things that you can go deeper into and become a partaker of. There is no need to be a taster when you can become a partaker!

1.   It means to become a partaker of Christ.

> Take care, brothers and sisters, that there will not be in any one of you an evil, unbelieving heart that falls away from the living God. But encourage one another every day, as long as it is still called "today," so that none of you will be hardened by the deceitfulness of sin. For we have become partakers of Christ if we keep the beginning of our commitment firm until the end, while it is said, "Today if you hear His voice, Do not harden your hearts, as when they provoked Me."
>
> Hebrews 3:12-15 (NASB)

Perhaps, the most important thing is for you to become a partaker of Christ. You must not only taste of the Lord to see that He is good. You must partake of Christ. To partake of Christ is to become deeply embedded and rooted in Him. You must go deeper and you must go all out in God.

Those who have partaken of salvation but have gone no deeper have made the greatest mistake of their lives. When I was a teenager in secondary school, many people claimed to be Christians. However, many did not take God seriously. They only tasted of the salvation but they did not partake of Christ. They did not go deeper into Christ as they should have. You must press on to the mark of the high calling of God. You must go deeper in Christ.

You cannot taste a bit and stop there. There is much more in Christ. It is because I pressed deeper into Christ that I became a pastor and a teacher of the Word. The sign that you have pressed on to be a partaker of Christ is that you have become a preacher and a teacher of the word of God. Indeed, there is a time that you must become a teacher of the Word.

> For when for the time ye ought to be teachers, ye have need that one teach you again which be the first principles of the oracles of God; and are become such as have need of milk, and not of strong meat.
>
> Hebrews 5:12

2.   It means to become a partaker of the divine nature.

> Grace and peace be multiplied to you in the knowledge of God and of Jesus our Lord, for His divine power has granted to us everything pertaining to life and godliness, through the true knowledge of Him who called us by His own glory and excellence. Through these He has granted to us His precious and magnificent promises, SO THAT BY THEM YOU MAY BECOME PARTAKERS OF THE DIVINE NATURE, having escaped the corruption that is in the world on account of lust.
>
> 2 Peter 1:2-4 (NASB)

The divine nature is the nature of God. You are expected to partake of the divine nature of God now that you are in Christ. Human beings are known to have a very evil nature. The nature of man is only set to get worse in the last days.

> This know also, that in the last days perilous times shall come. For men shall be lovers of their own selves, covetous, boasters, proud, blasphemers, disobedient to parents, unthankful, unholy, Without natural affection, trucebreakers, false accusers, incontinent, fierce, despisers of those that are good, Traitors, heady, highminded, lovers of pleasures more than lovers of God; Having a form of godliness, but denying the power thereof: from such turn away.
>
> 2 Timothy 3:1-5

For the wrath of God is revealed from heaven against all ungodliness and unrighteousness of men, who hold the truth in unrighteousness;

Because that which may be known of God is manifest in them; for God hath shewed it unto them.

For the invisible things of him from the creation of the world are clearly seen, being understood by the things that are made, even his eternal power and Godhead; so that they are without excuse:

Because that, when they knew God, they glorified him not as God, neither were thankful; but became vain in their imaginations, and their foolish heart was darkened.

Professing themselves to be wise, they became fools,

And changed the glory of the uncorruptible God into an image made like to corruptible man, and to birds, and fourfooted beasts, and creeping things.

Wherefore God also gave them up to uncleanness through the lusts of their own hearts, to dishonour their own bodies between themselves:

Who changed the truth of God into a lie, and worshipped and served the creature more than the Creator, who is blessed for ever. Amen.

For this cause God gave them up unto vile affections: for even their women did change the natural use into that which is against nature:

And likewise also the men, leaving the natural use of the woman, burned in their lust one toward another; men with men working that which is unseemly, and receiving in themselves that recompence of their error which was meet.

And even as they did not like to retain God in their knowledge, God gave them over to a reprobate mind, to do those things which are not convenient;

Being filled with all unrighteousness, fornication, wickedness, covetousness, maliciousness; full of envy, murder, debate, deceit, malignity; whisperers,

Backbiters, haters of God, despiteful, proud, boasters, inventors of evil things, disobedient to parents,

Without understanding, covenantbreakers, without natural affection, implacable, unmerciful:

Who knowing the judgment of God, that they which commit such things are worthy of death, not only do the same, but have pleasure in them that do them.

Romans 1:18-32

The evil nature of man is described in Romans 1 and 2 Timothy 3. Man has become depraved, perverse and wicked. You can expect even more wickedness in the last days as we approach the apocalyptic and cataclysmic conclusion of this world. When you come to Jesus, God gives you a new nature. If any man is in Christ, he is a new creature: old things are passed away; and all things are become new!

Apostle Paul teaches us to put on the nature of the new man. This new creation has a whole lot of new characteristics:

a) Instead of deception the new man is full of truth.

b) Instead of perpetual and unrelenting anger, the new man will have anger that lasts for a short time.

c) Instead of stealing, there will be hard work.

d) Instead of opening the door to the devil in many ways, all the entrances to demons will be shut tight.

e) Instead of continually grieving the Holy Spirit, you will be continually pleasing the Holy Spirit.

f) Instead of bitterness there will be forgiveness and love!

That, in reference to your former manner of life, you lay aside the old self, which is being corrupted in accordance with the lusts of deceit, and that you be renewed in the spirit of your mind, and put on the new self, which in the likeness of God has been created in righteousness and holiness of the truth. Therefore, laying aside falsehood, speak truth each one of you with his neighbor, for we are members of one another. Be angry, and yet do not sin; do not let the sun go down on your anger, and do not give the devil an opportunity. He who steals must steal no longer; but rather he must labor, performing with his own hands what is good, so that he will have something to share with one who has need. Let no unwholesome word proceed from your mouth, but only such a word as is good for edification according to the need of the moment, so that it will give grace to those who hear. Do not grieve the Holy Spirit of God, by whom you were sealed for the day of redemption. Let all bitterness and wrath and anger and clamor and slander be put away from you, along with all malice. Be kind to one another, tender-hearted, forgiving each other, just as God in Christ also has forgiven you.

Ephesians 4:22-32 (NASB)

You must become a partaker of this amazing divine nature. Today, many Christians are full of bitterness, anger, deception, lies and wickedness. Many Christians open the door to demons continually.

What does this mean? It means they have tasted of Christianity but have not become partakers of the divine nature. Becoming a partaker of the divine nature means that your nature has been blended into the character of Jesus Christ. Jesus Christ is full of love, patience and forgiveness. You will be full of love, patience and forgiveness when you become a partaker of the divine nature.

3.   It means to become a partaker of spiritual things.

But now I go unto Jerusalem to minister unto the saints. For it hath pleased them of Macedonia and Achaia to make a certain contribution for the poor saints which are at Jerusalem. It hath pleased them verily; and their debtors they are. For if the Gentiles have been made PARTAKERS OF THEIR SPIRITUAL THINGS, their duty is also to minister unto them in carnal things.

Romans 15:25-27

To be a partaker is to join yourself to something and become united with it.

The Gentiles have partaken of the spiritual blessings of Jews. There are people who are blessed with spiritual things and it is important to join yourself to them so that you can partake of the spiritual things that they have.

There is no point in just admiring great spiritual things that others have when you can actually be a partaker! What are some of the spiritual things that people have?

Some people have the spiritual grace to plant churches, to build churches and to send missionaries into the whole world. Standing on the outside, these things may seem extremely difficult to do. But sending missionaries to the world is a spiritual grace that some people have.

When I visited Dr. Cho's church in Korea, I discovered that they had sent missionaries to all parts of the world. They seemed to do it with ease. I met a Korean who spoke fluent Twi, a Ghanaian language, because his father had been a missionary in Ghana for some years. On the display boards, I saw pictures of Korean missionaries in almost every country of the world. This is in contrast with some churches that have one big church and no branches, no missionaries and no external international works. You can have some of the spiritual things that others have if you are prepared to pay the price.

We, the Gentiles, have joined ourselves and become united with Jews in their spiritual things. We are so united with them that we use the same holy book. The Torah, which is the Holy Book of the Jews is simply the Bible without the New Testament.

We are completely merged with Jews in our belief in Jehovah. We share with the Jews the God who saves, heals and delivers. That is what it means to become a partaker. When you become a partaker of another person's spiritual things, you will start to use his books, his videos and his audio messages. You will use the same tools and materials that he uses. Why do we use the same holy book as the Jews? Because we have become partakers of their spiritual things!

4. It means to become a partaker of the promises in Christ.

> For this reason I, Paul, the prisoner of Christ Jesus for the sake of you Gentiles — if indeed you have heard of the stewardship of God's grace which was given to me for you; that by revelation there was made known to me the mystery, as I wrote before in brief.
>
> By referring to this, when you read you can understand my insight into the mystery of Christ, which in other generations was not made known to the sons of men, as it has now been revealed to His holy apostles and prophets in the Spirit; to be specific, that the Gentiles are fellow heirs and fellow members of the body, and fellow PARTAKERS OF THE PROMISE IN CHRIST JESUS through the gospel, of which I was made a minister, according to the gift of God's grace which was given to me according to the working of His power.
>
> Ephesians 3:1-7 (NASB)

Instead of being a taster, you can become a partaker. To become a partaker is to go deeper and add yourself to the promises that are available to partakers. Tasters do not get a chance to partake of the promises made.

When you become a partaker of the promises of God, you are really a part of the family of God.

Becoming a partaker is to become completely merged and united with something. When you have bonded with a calling, a ministry or a family, you automatically begin to partake of the promises they enjoy.

God has called you to the ministry. Perhaps, He has given you someone to associate with, to merge with and to become bonded with. Why are you sitting on the fringes and only tasting? When you bond with someone, you bond with the promises that have been made to that person.

One day, I was praying and waiting on the Lord. I suddenly felt the Lord making a promise to me. He said to me, "I am going to give you a certain amount of money to build churches." The Lord mentioned a certain amount of money in United States dollars. Then He said He would give me a certain amount of money to do certain other things. If it is the case that God has promised me such huge amounts of money to build churches, then anyone who is completely merged with me and has become one with me and my ministry will receive part of this money for the building of churches.

When you are a partaker, you start to enjoy the benefits of promises that have been made to the person you have been joined to. I have some young men who are building cathedrals in foreign nations. They are spending huge amounts of money to develop their churches. This is because they are completely merged with me as part of my ministry. When I was their age, I did not have access to such monies to build churches. When I was their age, I resorted to raffles and begging millionaires for hand-outs to build the church. Since these young pastors have become part of my ministry, they are enjoying the huge amounts that were promised me for the ministry.

5.   **It means to become a partaker of an inheritance.**

Giving thanks unto the Father, which hath made us meet to be PARTAKERS OF THE INHERITANCE of the saints in light:

Colossians 1:12

You can also become a partaker of an inheritance. An inheritance is something that is passed on to you easily. Without any effort on your side, you suddenly become the owner of houses you did not build and properties you did not labour for.

You can actually merge yourself with another family and take part of their inheritance. I remember a young lady who was brought to a family when she was a little girl. She was actually the niece of the rich man. Even though she was not part of the biological family, when the father of the house died, he gave the lion's share of his property to this little girl. Of course, the rest of the family resented the fact that she had become a partaker of the inheritance.

One day, I met a man who said to me, "You are a part of my family." He said to me, "I want you to call me father. Do not call me any other name because I am your father." After knowing this man for some years, I was greatly impressed and I thought to myself, "I am now a son." I even went as far as to think that I would now be a partaker of the inheritance of this man and his family. In scripture, we are taught that we can actually take part in the inheritance of the saints.

I continued to see myself as a part of that family. I felt I was completely bonded, merged and entrenched in this family. However, it was not to be as I thought. When this man died, I was not a part of any inheritance whatsoever. Even the details of the inheritance became shrouded in mystery and I was excluded from all discussions on the inheritance.

Even though I felt that I had penetrated and become one with that family, it was not to the extent that I thought. It is not that easy to become a partaker of promises and of inheritance. You may feel close but are actually far away.

However, it is important to believe that you can receive your spiritual inheritance by blending yourself with the family of God.

There was a millionaire who used to go to a restaurant to eat. He was widowed and lonely and used to spend a lot of his time at the restaurant. There was a seventeen-year-old girl who worked at the restaurant as a part time waitress. This lonely widower would eat lunch and dinner there every day. The employees of the restaurant and some customers virtually became his family. If he were late for a meal, this waitress would call him to make sure he was all right. The waitress began running errands for this old man and helping him in his house. Because of his poor eyesight, she often helped him to read his mails and pay his bills. As this kind waitress got deeper into the life of the old man, she became a partaker of his wealth. When he died, he left the little girl a fortune. She had become a partaker of his inheritance.

It is not so easy to become a partaker of an inheritance. Indeed, it is one of the highest signs of partaking if you are ever given an inheritance by someone who is not your biological parent.

6. It means to become a partaker of the grace of God.

I thank my God upon every remembrance of you, always in every prayer of mine for you all making request with joy, For your fellowship in the gospel from the first day until now; Being confident of this very thing, that he which hath begun a good work in you will perform it until the day of Jesus Christ: Even as it is meet for me to think this of you all, because I have you in my heart; inasmuch as both in my bonds, and in the defence and confirmation of the gospel, YE ALL ARE PARTAKERS OF MY GRACE.

Philippians 1:3-7

You can become a partaker of someone's grace. Paul said, "You are all partakers of my grace." What was Paul's grace? Grace is the abundant help of God that is given to you to accomplish something. When people are walking in grace, they do things easily. Whatever Paul accomplished with ease was what the grace of God allowed him to.

Every man of God has a grace that is given to him. One day I heard a man of God describing how he had built forty-four boarding schools in one year. These schools included classrooms and dormitories for the accommodation of the students. I was amazed because I had been trying to build one school for many years. Whenever someone is walking in a grace, he seems to do amazing things with ease.

It is possible to be a partaker of someone's grace so that you can do amazing things with ease. Perhaps someone has the grace to pray for many hours. Perhaps, someone has the grace to preach for many hours.

Someone once told me that I had the grace to preach for a long time. I had never thought of myself as someone who preaches for long because I have never intended to preach for a long time. Actually, I prefer to preach for a short time. It is much more restful for me.

Then I met someone who said to me, "We started the meeting at 9.00am this morning and we closed at 9.00pm. You preached from this morning to this evening and we were not tired of listening to you. That alone should tell you about the grace of God that is on your life."

Whatever someone does easily is a grace that has been given to him. Grace is undeserved help from God. You can be united to and join yourself to someone else's grace. You can become involved with someone else's grace. You can even be a component or part of that grace.

King David had the grace to fight and to win his battles. David even had the grace to kill giants. Many of the people who walked with David partook of his grace to kill giants. Sibbecai the Hushathite killed Sippai the giant. Elhanan the son of Jair killed Lahmi, Goliath's brother. Jonathan the nephew of David also killed a giant who taunted Israel. The grace to kill giants was on all of King David's assistants.

> He brought out the people who were in it, and cut them with saws and with sharp instruments and with axes. And thus David did to all the cities of the sons of Ammon. Then David and all the people returned to Jerusalem. Now it came about after this, that war broke out at Gezer with the Philistines; then SIBBECAI THE HUSHATHITE KILLED SIPPAI, ONE OF THE DESCENDANTS OF THE GIANTS, and they were subdued. And there was war with the Philistines again, and ELHANAN THE SON OF JAIR KILLED LAHMI THE BROTHER OF GOLIATH THE GITTITE, the shaft of whose spear was like a weaver's beam. Again there was war at Gath, where there was a man of great stature who had twenty-four fingers

and toes, six fingers on each hand and six toes on each foot; and he also was descended from the giants. WHEN HE TAUNTED ISRAEL, JONATHAN THE SON OF SHIMEA, DAVID'S BROTHER, KILLED HIM. These were descended from the giants in Gath, and they fell by the hand of David and by the hand of his servants.

1 Chronicles 20:3-8 (NASB)

Indeed, you can be a partaker of someone else's grace. To be a partaker of a grace is to be completely merged and amalgamated into that grace. You will do with ease what that grace gives you the ability to do.

There is a grace for the prophetic ministry.

One day, I saw a prophet demonstrating amazing gifts of prophecy with amazing words of knowledge. He was calling out details of people's bankcards, car numbers and house numbers. I was amazed as he operated in his gift. To my amazement his son was also walking in the same gift. His wife also seemed to be walking in this gift. His associate pastors also seemed to be prophets, having similar gifts. I realised that this man had certain spiritual things that I did not have. No one in my world had these spiritual gifts. It is possible to rise and partake of spiritual things that others have. If you are humble and ready to learn, you can become a partaker of spiritual things that other people have.

7. It means to be a partaker of a heavenly calling.

Therefore, holy brethren, PARTAKERS OF A HEAVENLY CALLING, consider Jesus, the Apostle and High Priest of our confession. He was faithful to Him who appointed Him, as Moses also was in all His house.

Hebrews 3:1-2 (NASB)

You can also be a partaker of someone's divine call. Being a partaker of someone's calling means that you become one with that heavenly calling! It also means that you gain access into the work of the ministry and play a part in the ministry yourself.

Many people are not actually called to the ministry themselves but are simply partakers of someone else's calling. Being a partaker of someone else's calling means that you have become involved with the ministry. You can be merged and amalgamated into someone's divine call.

For many people, the only way to do the ministry is to join themselves to someone who has a heavenly calling. When you join yourself to someone who has a divine call, it will seem as though you have a heavenly calling too.

Unfortunately, many people who are working with a man of God become presumptuous and think they also have a calling. Notice what Miriam and Aaron said: "Hath the LORD indeed spoken only by Moses? hath he not spoken also by us? And the LORD heard it. (Now the man Moses was very meek, above all the men which were upon the face of the earth.)" (Numbers 12:2-3)

Miriam and Aaron challenged Moses, claiming to also be called. All of us who read the books of Moses can clearly see that it was Moses whom God had called. Korah, Dathan and Abiram also challenged Moses about his calling. They did not learn their lessons from what happened to Miriam and Aaron.

> "Now Korah, the son of Izhar, the son of Kohath, the son of Levi, and Dathan and Abiram, the sons of Eliab, and On, the son of Peleth, sons of Reuben, took men: And they rose up before Moses, with certain of the children of Israel, two hundred and fifty princes of the assembly, famous in the congregation, men of renown: And they gathered themselves together against Moses and against Aaron, and said unto them, Ye take too much upon you, seeing all the congregation are holy, every one of them, and the LORD is among them: wherefore then lift ye up yourselves above the congregation of the LORD? And when Moses heard it, he fell upon his face:" (Numbers 16:1-4)

If God has chosen that you should be a part of someone's heavenly calling, do not make a mistake in jumping out of the ship. You will regret it because without your own calling you will amount to nothing.

8. It means to become a partaker of the anointing.

> Therefore leaving the elementary teaching about the Christ, let us press on to maturity, not laying again a foundation of repentance from dead works and of faith toward God, of instruction about washings, and laying on of hands, and the resurrection of the dead, and eternal judgment.
>
> And this we shall do, if God permits.
>
> For in the case of those who have once been enlightened and have tasted of the heavenly gift and have been made PARTAKERS OF THE HOLY SPIRIT, and have tasted the good word of God and the powers of the age to come, and then have fallen away, it is impossible to renew them again to repentance, since they again crucify to themselves the Son of God, and put Him to open shame.
>
> Hebrews 6:1-6 (NASB)

You can become a partaker of the anointing of the Holy Spirit. As the scripture above teaches, you can become a partaker of the anointing.

The anointing of the Holy Spirit can be shared. God spoke to Moses and said He would come down from heaven and take the spirit that was upon Moses and share it to the seventy elders.

> And the Lord said unto Moses, Gather unto me seventy men of the elders of Israel, whom thou knowest to be the elders of the people, and officers over them; and bring them unto the tabernacle of the congregation, that they may stand there with thee. And I will come down and talk with thee there: and I will take of the spirit which is upon

thee, and will put it upon them; and they shall bear the burden of the people with thee, that thou bear it not thyself alone.

Numbers 11:16-17

The seventy elders partook of the ministry of Moses. The seventy elders were completely merged into Moses's ministry. The seventy elders became a part of Moses' ministry. The seventy elders bore the burden of Moses' ministry. The seventy elders imitated Moses because they were united with him.

You can be joined to someone's anointing. The Holy Spirit is the basis for all ministry. If you have eyes to see, you will recognize that no one can accomplish much with his natural strength. The power of God is necessary to make anything out of your ministry.

If you participate in someone's ministry and are committed to it, you can merge into the anointing that the person is carrying.

By involving yourself and joining yourself with people who are anointed, you become anointed too. Jesus asked His disciples to simply follow Him so that they would become anointed too.

You can partake of the anointing by becoming bonded and united with someone who is heavily anointed. Why do you think Elisha followed Elijah for so many years? You never hear of Elijah praying for Elisha! You never hear of Elijah laying hands on Elisha! When Elijah tried to get rid of Elisha before he was caught up to heaven, Elisha would have none of it. He considered himself to be completely bonded and merged with Elijah. There was no way he was going to separate from him. Elijah tried four times to sack Elisha but Elisha simply said, "I am completely merged and amalgamated into you." Sending me away will not work. I am bonded and united with you!

This is what it means to become a partaker of someone else's anointing. Elisha partook of the great anointing that was on Elijah. You can do that too!

9.   It means to be a become partakers of chastisement.

> If ye endure chastening, God dealeth with you as with sons; for what son is he whom the father chasteneth not? But if ye be without chastisement, whereof all are partakers, then are ye bastards, and not sons.
>
> Hebrews 12:7-8

You must be a partaker of chastisement when it falls to you. If you do not taste of the chastisement, then you are not a son. The scripture is clear. You can either be a taster or a partaker. There are some people who will accept punishment up to a point. After a certain point they say, "This is nonsense. I can't take this any more. What is the point in suffering so much?" But the scripture is clear. If you endure chastening, God dealeth with you as sons. If you are without chastisement whereof all are partakers, then you are bastards.

To be a partaker of chastisement means that you have entrusted yourself to the Father and believe that all that He is taking you through is for your good. To be a partaker of chastisement means that you are committed wholly to your Father and He can do anything to punish or restrict you.

Because people are not completely bonded to their spiritual fathers, they are easily separated by a rebuke, a correction or any form of punishment. When you have joined yourself to something and are merged into it, nothing can separate you from it.

You must be able to receive repeated corrections and rebukes. The Bible is full of instructions for the man of God to reprove, to rebuke and to correct people.

> Them that sin REBUKE before all, that others also may fear.
>
> 1 Timothy 5:20

Preach the word; be instant in season, out of season; REPROVE, REBUKE, exhort with all longsuffering and doctrine.

2 Timothy 4:2

Through your ability to partake in chastisement and rebukes, many blessings of the house will also fall to you.

10. It means to be a partaker of the sufferings and of the glory.

But rejoice, inasmuch as ye are partakers of Christ's sufferings; that, when his glory shall be revealed, ye may be glad also with exceeding joy.

1 Peter 4:13

The elders which are among you I exhort, who am also an elder, and a witness of the sufferings of Christ, and also a partaker of the glory that shall be revealed:

1 Peter 5:1

Suffering is always followed by glory. If you are deep into the sufferings, you will receive the glory. You must decide to completely blend into the sufferings of Christ. There is suffering in the ministry because we are called to suffer as well as to believe in God.

When people run away from the suffering, they are also inadvertently running away from the glory of God. The reasons why many people avoid full-time ministry is because they do not want to suffer any loss for Jesus Christ. If you lose your life for Jesus, you will gain it. If you suffer for Christ, you will receive glory.

By running away from any form of suffering whatsoever, you are fleeing from your greatest blessings in Christ. Remember that Jesus Christ is worthy to receive glory and honour and power and riches and blessing because He endured the cross and suffered the shame for us. How will you ever be worthy to receive glory and honour and power and riches and blessing if you are not prepared to endure your cross?

It is time to be a partaker and to enter into the "suffering" aspect of serving God. You must identify with and completely merge yourself into the ministry and whatever it holds for you. Do not be an outsider! Do not be an onlooker! Be a partaker!

One of my bishops was insulted by a rebellious and deceived Christian. This same rebellious and deceived Christian had been insulting me for some time. Like a rabid dog that had gone insane, he turned on anyone who objected to his defamatory, calumnious, malicious and wicked utterances. My dear bishop received the full brunt of this rabid individual's wrath. He called me, full of joy and rejoicing and said to me, "I am so glad that I received some of the insults that you have been receiving. I feel so honoured that I have also been insulted."

> The Lord give mercy unto the house of Onesiphorus; for he oft refreshed me, and was not ashamed of my chain: But, when he was in Rome, he sought me out very diligently, and found me. The Lord grant unto him that he may find mercy of the Lord in that day: and in how many things he ministered unto me at Ephesus, thou knowest very well.
>
> 2 Timothy 1:16-18

Onesiphorus was not ashamed of Paul's chains but identified with Paul's shame and disgrace.

It is important to identify with the shame and disgrace that is associated with ministry. God has a plan for you. Immerse yourself into His will. Do not stand on the fringes and taste of the ministry without partaking in the sufferings.

You are promised glory after you have been a partaker of the sufferings. "For our light affliction, which is but for a moment, worketh for us a far more exceeding and eternal weight of glory;" (2 Corinthians 4:17).

Every affliction that you experience now is working out some glory for you. Do you want to receive the glory of God in your life? Do you want to see His beauty? Do you want your life to be beautiful? Then fully embrace the sufferings of Jesus Christ. Be like Onesiphorus and do not be ashamed of the ministry and of God's servant.

God is going to bless you mightily with His glory as you serve Him and fully accept to be immersed into whatever sufferings, shame, calumny, slander, defamation, horror or pain inflicted on you. God is great! At the end of the day, you will enjoy His glory.

Conclusion

Dear friend, you have heard what it is to be a taster. You have seen many things that you can partake of. Decide to go deeper and do more!

To the making of many books, there is simply no end! With these few words, I pray you will arise from the level of a taster and become a partaker of the great things God has for you.